HEART HEALTHY DIET COOKBOOK FOR SENIORS

The Quick and Easy Guide to Managing Blood Pressure problems, with Low-sodium Recipes + 30 day meal plan.

MALONEY DEAN

Copyright © 2023 by MALONEY DEAN

All rights reserved

No part of this publication may be reproduced, distributed, or transmitted in any form or by any means, including photocopying, recording, or other electronic or mechanical methods, without the prior written permission of the publisher, except in the case of brief quotations embodied in critical reviews and certain other noncommercial uses permitted by copyright law.

OTHER BOOKS BY THE SAME AUTHORS

VEGAN DIET FOR SENIORS WITH CHRONIC KIDNEY DISEASE

MEDITERRANEAN DIET RECIPES FOR SENIORS

TABLE OF CONTENTS

INTRODUCTION

CHAPTER 1: HEART HEALTHY DIET RECIPES

1. Oatmeal with Berries and Nuts
2. Greek Yogurt Parfait
3. Whole Grain Pancakes
4. Fruity Smoothie Bowl
5. Morning Glory Muffins
6. Hearty Lentil Soup
7. Classic Minestrone Soup
8. Spinach and Walnut Salad
9. Baked Salmon with Dill Sauce
10. Lemon Herb Grilled Chicken
11. Vegetable Stir-Fry with Tofu
12. Lentil and Vegetable Stew
13. Quinoa and Black Bean Burgers
14. Garlic Mashed Cauliflower
15. Roasted Sweet Potatoes
16. Whole Grain Pilaf
17. Steamed Broccoli with Lemon and parmesan
18. Sauteed Spinach with Garlic
19. Hummus and Veggie Platter
20. Guacamole with Whole Wheat Pita

21. Trail Mix base recipe with Nuts and Seeds
22. Stuffed Bell Peppers
23. Avocado and Tomato Bruschetta
24. Fresh Fruit Salad with Mint
25. Banana-Oat Cookies
26. Berry Crisp with Almond Topping
27. Dark Chocolate-Dipped Strawberries
28. Baked Apples with Cinnamon
29. Quinoa and Vegetable Stir-Fry
30. Grilled Shrimp and Asparagus Skewers
31. Sweet Potato and Black Bean Quesadillas
32. Cucumber and Dill Greek Salad
33. Berry and Almond Overnight Oats
34. Mediterranean Chickpea Salad
35. Spinach and Artichoke Stuffed Chicken Breast
36. Cauliflower Fried Rice
37. Tomato Basil Mozzarella Salad
38. Salmon and Quinoa Stuffed Bell Peppers
39. Vegetarian Lentil Loaf
40. Cabbage and White Bean Soup

BONUS RECIPE

41. Lemon Garlic Shrimp Pasta

CONCLUSION

30 Day Meal Planner

INTRODUCTION

My father struggled with his meals after the demise of his beloved wife in 2021. He had developed high blood pressure as a result of the grief and pains of losing his beloved wife of 28 years.

He began to long for his favorite meals but because of his heart issues, he couldn't eat his favorite meals and snacks.

The Doctor had restricted him to bland, unexciting foods and he was missing out on good foods.

His struggles with nutritious healthy meals continued until i came home from vacation and spent a month with him.

I introduced him to delicious, healthy cuisine that were heart friendly and also delicious and highly nutritious.

He watched me as i started experimenting with new recipes, ingredients, and snacks.

After a while, he joined me and started taking notes and before long, he had become a master in the preparation of healthy heart healthy mediterranean diets.

And most importantly, his health improved tremendously and his blood pressure stabilized.

I wrote this book when i realized the extent of the health crises on our hands in this country and how lots of our senior citizens are suffering from heart related diseases that has negatively impacted their lives and careers.

This book is the solution you seek

Now you can finally enjoy delicious meals while making sure you feed your system with nutritious meals that are heart friendly.

In the pages that follow, you will find exciting heart friendly recipes, the ingredients, preparation methods, and other information you need to turn your kitchen into a sanctuary of culinary bliss.

CHAPTER 1: HEART HEALTHY DIET RECIPES

1. Oatmeal with Berries and Nuts

Oats are heart-healthy meals. They are naturally gluten-free.

They are also low in fat, rich in protein and are full of soluble fiber that keeps your gut bacteria happy and your cholesterol reasonably down.

Oats are rich in essential like manganese, selenium, phosphorus, fiber, magnesium, and zinc.

And when combined with berries and nuts, the taste is heavenly.

Ingredients:

- ✓ Half cup of rolled oats
- ✓ One cup of almond milk
- ✓ Half cup of mixed berries
- ✓ Two tablespoons of chopped nuts (walnuts or almonds)

Preparation:

Start by Cooking the oats with almond milk.

Then Top it with mixed berries and then chopped nuts.

Nutritional Value:

Calories: 300

Fiber: 8g

Protein: 10g

Preparation Time: 10 minutes

2. Greek Yogurt Parfait

Ingredients:

- ✓ One cup of Greek yogurt
- ✓ Half a cup of granola

- ✓ Half cup of fresh fruit (e.g., sliced strawberries)

Preparation:

Build the yogurt parfait layers: Start by Spooning half of the yogurt at the bottom of a bowl, or mason jar.

Proceed to layer with half of the fruit (sliced strawberries) and half of the granola.

For the remaining yogurt mixture, carefully spoon it into the glass and then add the rest of the fruit and granola to the top.

To add additional flavor, finish it with a drizzle of honey (or maple syrup).

You can add more fresh fruit, and granola on top.

Serve immediately or store in the refrigerator for later consumption.

Nutritional Value:

Calories: 250

Protein: 15g

Calcium: 20%

Preparation Time: 7 minutes

3. Whole Grain Pancakes

Ingredients:
- One cup of whole wheat flour
- One tablespoon of baking powder
- One cup of skim milk
- One egg

Preparation:

Mix all the ingredients, then cook them on a griddle.

Nutritional Value:

Calories: 200

Fiber: 5g

Protein: 8g

Preparation Time: 15 minutes

4. Fruity Smoothie Bowl

Ingredients:

One frozen banana

Half cup of mixed berries

Half cup of spinach

Half cup of almond milk

Preparation:

Blend all the ingredients together until they become smooth.

Then proceed to top it with additional berries.

Nutritional Value:

Calories: 180

Vitamin C: 30%

Iron: 10%

Preparation Time: 5 minutes

5. Morning Glory Muffins

Ingredients:

- ✓ One cup of grated carrots
- ✓ Half cup of unsweetened applesauce
- ✓ One quarter cup of chopped nuts
- ✓ One cup of whole wheat flour

Preparation:

Mix all the ingredients together. Then bake in a muffin tin.

Nutritional Value:

Calories: 150

Fiber: 4g

Vitamin A: 50%

Preparation Time: 18 minutes

6. Hearty Lentil Soup

This delicious lentil soup recipe is thick and also filling.

You will enjoy it because it's hearty, healthy, vegan and gluten-free

It is a perfect meal for lunch!

Ingredients:

- ✓ Two tablespoons of olive oil
- ✓ One cup of dried brown lentils
- ✓ One onion then diced
- ✓ Two stalks celery
- ✓ One garlic
- ✓ One Lemon
- ✓ Two carrots. Then chop them up
- ✓ Four cups of vegetable broth

Preparation:

Place a soup pot on the stove top and then set the heat to medium high.

Add Two Tablespoon of olive oil to the pot.

Once the oil is well heated, go ahead to add the garlic, onions, and celery to the olive oil on fire.

Sauté the aromatics for about 5 minutes. Ensure you stir occasionally.

Add the carrots to the pot, along with One quarter tablespoon of each of kosher salt and pepper.

Sauté the carrots for about 5. stir occasionally.

Add One and quarter cup of brown lentils to the pot and sauté for One minute. Stir occasionally.

Nutritional Value:

Calories: 220

Protein: 15g

Fiber: 10g

Preparation Time: 25 minutes

7. Classic Minestrone Soup

Minestrone is a hearty and healthy Italian vegetable soup. It is made with tomato-y broth and either pasta or rice.

Ingredients:

- ✓ Three tablespoons of olive oil
- ✓ One onion
- ✓ One can of diced tomatoes
- ✓ One cup of whole wheat pasta
- ✓ Two cups of mixed vegetables
- ✓ Four cups of vegetable broth

Preparation:

STEP ONE

Heat the olive oil in a medium-sized saucepan over a heal level that is medium.

The proceed to fry the onion, celery, carrot, courgetti and pancetta gently for about 10 minutes.

Add the garlic and oregano, and cook for One more min.

Add the beans, the chopped tomatoes, purée, stock and bay leaf.

Add salt and pepper for added flavor and to season the meal.

Bring to the simmer and cook for 25 mins.

STEP TWO

Add the pasta and greens to the pot.

Cook for a further 12 minutes.

Ladle into the bowls, then proceed to scatter with the basil and some of the parmesan

Then simmer the tomatoes, pasta, vegetables, and broth.

Nutritional Value:

Calories: 180

Fiber: 8g

Vitamin C: 25%

Preparation Time: 25 minutes

8. *Spinach and Walnut Salad*

Walnuts add some tasty crunch to this easy and delicious spinach salad.

I love it flavored with honey, orange and a hint of cinnamon, it will surely spice up and make your day and.

Ingredients:

- ✓ Two cups of fresh spinach
- ✓ One quarter cup of finely chopped walnuts
- ✓ Half cup of cherry tomatoes
- ✓ two tablespoons of balsamic vinaigrette

Preparation:

STEP ONE

Put the walnuts in a medium pan. Set the heat to medium and cook.

Stir for three minutes or until it becomes golden.

Transfer to a chopping board and coarsely them finely chop.

STEP TWO

Blend the ingredients together in a small bowl - the orange juice, oil, honey, garlic and cinnamon.

Spice up the taste and season with salt and pepper.

STEP THREE

Put the spinach and walnut in a serving bowl.

Trickle over the dressing and toss to combine.

Then Serve.

Nutritional Value:

Calories: 120

Vitamin K: 50%

Antioxidants: High

Preparation time: 60 minutes

9. Baked Salmon with Dill Sauce

I love to pair the baked salmon with fresh and easy yogurt-based dill sauce.

It could be made in about 30 minutes.

And you will absolutely love how simple, easy to prepare and flavorful this dill sauce and salmon is.

Ingredients:

- ✓ Two salmon fillets
- ✓ One tablespoon of olive oil
- ✓ One tablespoon of chopped fresh dill
- ✓ One lemon. Then slice it

Preparation:

Set the oven heat to 400°F (200°C).

Then proceed to place the salmon onto the baking sheet.

Trickle over with olive oil, and sprinkle with chopped dill.

Then proceed to arrange the lemon slices on top of the salmon.

Cook for about 20 minutes or until the salmon is cooked through.

Nutritional Value:

Calories: 250

Protein: 25g

Omega-3 Fatty Acids: 1.5g

Preparation Time: 25 minutes

10. Lemon Herb Grilled Chicken

You'll absolutely love this simple lemon marinade on this grilled chicken!

It's so easy to prepare, flavorful and delicious.

Ingredients:

- ✓ Two boneless and skinless chicken breasts
- ✓ Two tablespoons of lemon juice
- ✓ One teaspoon of dried herbs (e.g., thyme, rosemary)

Preparation:

Set the grill heat to medium-high heat.

Soak the chicken breast in lemon juice and dried herbs for at least 30 minutes.

Cook the chicken on the grill about 7 minutes per side or until it is well cooked.

Nutritional Value:

Calories: 180

Protein: 30g

Vitamin C: 10% DV

Preparation Time: 35 minutes (including the marination)

11. Vegetable Stir-Fry with Tofu

Ingredients:

- ✓ One cup of tofu. Then cut into cubes
- ✓ Two cups of mixed vegetables (e.g., broccoli, bell peppers, snap peas)
- ✓ Fresh garlic and ginger
- ✓ Two tablespoons of soy sauce
- ✓ One tablespoon of sesame oil

Preparation:

Start by heating the sesame oil in a frying pan over high heat.

Add the tofu and stir-fry until it becomes golden brown.

Then proceed to add the mixed vegetables, garlic, ginger and soy sauce.

Continue to stir-fry until the vegetables are becomes soft and tender.

Nutritional Value:

Calories: 220

Protein: 15g

Fiber: 8g

Preparation Time: 20 minutes

12. Lentil and Vegetable Stew

This is a mediterranean recipes that is excellent for dinner.

This lentil stew is heart-healthy and easy to make.

It is loaded with vegetables, spices, and delicious fresh herbs.

Ingredients:

- ✓ One cup of dried green lentils
- ✓ Two carrots, then diced
- ✓ zucchini squash
- ✓ One Celery stalk
- ✓ 1 diced tomatoes
- ✓ One finely chopped onion
- ✓ Four cups of vegetable broth
- ✓ Two cloves of garlic. Then mince it

Preparation:

Wash the lentils and cover with water.

Soak for about 12 minutes.

Drain the water and pick out the stones

Combine them with the chopped carrots, onion, garlic and vegetable broth in a pot.

Simmer over medium heat for another 25 minutes or until the lentils are soft.

Nutritional Value:

Calories: 230

Protein: 15g

Fiber: 12g

Preparation Time: 35 minutes

13. Quinoa and Black Bean Burgers

These vegetarian black bean and quinoa burgers recipes are delicious!

Your meat loving friends will be so impressed.

My favorite way to serve this delicious meal is on a whole wheat bun with garlic-lemon mayonnaise with fresh spinach leaves, sliced tomato, and onions.

Ingredients:

- ✓ One cup of cooked quinoa
- ✓ One can of black beans, rinsed and mashed
- ✓ Half cup of breadcrumbs
- ✓ One teaspoon of grounded cumin

- ✓ One large egg
- ✓ One cove of garlic, then mince it
- ✓ One teaspoon of salt to taste
- ✓ Three tablespoon of olive oil
- ✓ One teaspoon of pepper sauce

Preparation:

In a pan, bring the quinoa to a boil with water

Bring the heat down and simmer until quinoa is soft and the water is fully absorbed.

Mashed the black beans with fork.

Mix the quinoa, breadcrumbs, pepper, egg, onion, salt and cumin.

Form the mixture into patties and bake in the oven at a heat of 375°F (190°C) for about 20 minutes.

Then proceed to heat the olive oil in a large frying pan

Cook the patties in hot oil until it is thoroughly heated for about 5 minutes on every side.

Nutritional Value:

Calories: 180

Protein: 10g

Fiber: 8g

Preparation Time: 30 minutes

14. Garlic Mashed Cauliflower

Ingredients:

- ✓ One head of chopped cauliflower
- ✓ Two cloves minced garlic
- ✓ Two tablespoons of olive oil
- ✓ Parmesan and cream cheese
- ✓ Salt and pepper to taste

Preparation:

Steam cauliflower until it becomes soft.

Then cook the garlic in the olive oil

Mash the cooked cauliflower and blend in the minced garlic, olive oil, salt, and pepper.

Nutritional Value:

Calories: 120

Fiber: 6g

Vitamin C: 80% DV

Preparation Time: 25 minutes

15. Roasted Sweet Potatoes

Sweet potatoes are one of the most nutrients densed vegetables out there. This recipe brings out the best in them

Ingredients:

- ✓ Two sweet potatoes, then cubed
- ✓ One tablespoon of olive oil
- ✓ One teaspoon of smoked paprika
- ✓ Cumin, Paprika and garlic
- ✓ Add Salt and pepper to taste

Preparation:

Set the heat of the oven to 425°F (220°C).

Toss the sweet potatoes with olive oil, smoked paprika, salt, and pepper.

Roast them in the oven for about 30 minutes or until it becomes golden and crispy.

Nutritional Value:

Calories: 150

Fiber: 4g

Vitamin A: 400% DV

Preparation Time: 30 minutes

16. Whole Grain Pilaf

Ingredients:

- ✓ One cup of mixed whole grains (e.g., quinoa, brown rice, farro)
- ✓ Two cups of vegetable broth

- ✓ Red bell pepper
- ✓ Salt to taste
- ✓ One quarter cup of chopped fresh herbs (e.g., parsley, thyme)

Preparation:

Combine the mixed whole grains and vegetable broth in a pot.

Bring to a boil.

Then simmer until grains becomes soft.

Blend and stir in in the fresh herbs, salt and pepper before serving.

Nutritional Value:

Calories: 200

Protein: 8g

Fiber: 10g

Preparation Time: 25 minutes

17. Steamed Broccoli with Lemon and parmesan

Ingredients:

- Two cups of broccoli florets
- One tablespoon of lemon juice
- One teaspoon of olive oil
- Garlic powder (optional)

Preparation:

Steam the broccoli until it becomes crisp-soft.

Then mix in the lemon juice, olive oil, and garlic powder.

Nutritional Value:

Calories: 50

Protein: 3g

Fiber: 4g

Vitamin C: 90% DV

Preparation Time: 20 minutes

18. Sauteed Spinach with Garlic

Ingredients:

- Four cups of fresh spinach
- Two cloves of garlic. Then mince it
- One tablespoon of olive oil
- Add Salt and pepper to taste

Preparation:

Start by heating the olive oil in a frying pan over medium heat.

Add the minced garlic and fry gently until the fragrance comes out well

Add the fresh spinach, toss until wilted.

Then season with salt and pepper.

Nutritional Value:

Calories: 80

Protein: 5g

Fiber: 4g

Preparation Time: 10 minutes

19. Hummus and Veggie Platter

Ingredients:
- One cup of hummus
- Assorted vegetable sticks (carrots, cucumbers, bell peppers)
- Three cups of Broccoli Florets
- One Pints of Grape tomatoes

Preparation:

Arrange hummus in a small bowl in the center of a platter.

Place the assorted vegetable sticks in a circle on platter for dipping.

Nutritional Value:

Calories: 150

Protein: 6g

Fiber: 8g

Potassium: 325mg

Sodium: 140mg

Preparation Time: 10 minutes

20. Guacamole with Whole Wheat Pita

This guacamole with whole wheat pita recipe is a super easy heart-healthy vegan recipe to prepare.

All you need do is just mash the avocados in a bowl and mix in the chopped ingredients.

It pairs perfectly with some homemade pita chips.

I love it as a snack or appetizer especially when i have an extra avocado kicking around the kitchen and don't want them to go bad.

Ingredients:

- Two ripe avocados, mashed
- One tomato. Then dice it
- One quarter cup of red onion. Then chop it nicely
- One lime. Then juice it
- Two tablespoons of garlic. Then mince it
- Include Salt and pepper to taste
- Whole wheat pita for serving

Preparation:

Set the oven heat to 325f.

Then proceed to cut each of the pita into 8 equal triangles

Place the 8 pitas on baking steel.

Bake this for about Ten Minutes

In a bowl, mix in the mashed avocados, diced tomato, lime juice, chopped red onion, salt, and pepper.

Serve with whole pita chips.

Nutritional Value:

Calories: 200

Protein: 5g

Fiber: 8g

Preparation Time: 15 minutes

21. Trail Mix base recipe with Nuts and Seeds

Trail mix base recipe doesn't need a lot of ingredients to prepare.

It only requires just 1 simple step, so it's a great recipe to practice customizing to your taste!

You will love to mix, stir and shake the ingredients together.

Ingredients:

- ✓ Half cup of almonds
- ✓ Half cup of walnuts
- ✓ One quarter cup of pumpkin seeds
- ✓ One quarter cup of dried cranberries
- ✓ One quarter cup of dark chocolate chips

Preparation:

Mix in all the above stated ingredients in a bowl.

Mix them well and apportion them into snack-sized bags.

Nutritional Value:

Calories: 250

Protein: 7g

Fiber: 5g

Preparation Time: 5 minutes

22. *Stuffed Bell Peppers*

Ingredients:

- ✓ Four bell peppers. Cut them into halves
- ✓ One cup of quinoa, cooked
- ✓ One can of black beans. Grain and rinse it
- ✓ One cup of corn kernels
- ✓ One cup of salsa
- ✓ Half tablespoon of garlic powder
- ✓ One cup of marinata sauce
- ✓ One cup of chicken broth
- ✓ Half cup of uncooked long grain white rice
- ✓ One teaspoon of cumin

Preparation:

Set the oven heat to 375°F (190°C).

In a bowl, mix cooked quinoa, black beans, corn, salsa, and cumin.

Wash, dry each of the bell pepper

The cut the bell peppers into halves.

Brush each of the bell peppers with One tablespoon of oil

Season with salt and black pepper

Proceed to bake the bell peppers for another 12 minutes.

While baking the bell peppers, heat a medium sized frying pan over medium heat.

Add One tablespoon of olive oil. Brown the italian sausage

Add the diced onions and garlic as well to the frying pan.

Saute on the frying pan until the fragrance comes out well.

Proceed to add the uncooked rice, marinara sauce, italian seasoning and the garlic powder

Add One tablespoon of salt and the chicken broth to the frying pan.

Stir very well and cook for another 25 minutes

Fill each of the bell pepper with meat filling

Bake the bell peppers for another 15 minutes so the bell pepper becomes soft.

Nutritional Value:

Calories: 220

Protein: 10g

Fiber: 8g

Preparation Time: 45 minutes

23. Avocado and Tomato Bruschetta

Ingredients:

- ✓ Two ripe avocados. Then dice it

- ✓ 1One cup of cherry tomatoes. Cut into halves
- ✓ One quarter cup of red onion.
- ✓ Chop them up nicely
- ✓ Fresh basil leaves for garnish
- ✓ Garlic powder
- ✓ lemon juice
- ✓ Whole grain baguette slices

Preparation:

In a bowl, mix in the diced avocados, cherry tomatoes, chopped red onion, and lemon juice.

Spoon the mixture onto whole grain baguette slices.

Embellish it with fresh basil leaves.

Nutritional Value:

Calories: 180

Protein: 5g

Fiber: 7g

Preparation Time: 15 minutes

24. Fresh Fruit Salad with Mint

If you are lover of fruit salads, especially one that is easy to make, then this colorful combination of assorted fruits and drizzled with honey will surely make your day.

Ingredients:

- ✓ Two cups of mixed fresh fruit (e.g., berries, melon, pineapple)
- ✓ Two tablespoons of fresh mint. Then chop it
- ✓ One tablespoon of honey
- ✓ Orange juice
- ✓ Large mint leaves

Preparation:

Wash and chop the fresh fruits

Place them in a medium sized bowl.

Sprinkle it with honey and also add the chopped mint leaves on top.

Toss everything together

Nutritional Value:

Calories: 120

Fiber: 5g

Vitamin C: 80% DV

Preparation Time: 12 minutes

25. Banana-Oat Cookies

This banana oatmeal is delicious and perfect for any time of the day

Ingredients:
- ✓ Two ripe bananas. mash them

- ✓ One cup of rolled oats
- ✓ One quarter cup of almond butter
- ✓ One quarter cup of dark chocolate chips
- ✓ One teaspoon of vanilla extract

Preparation:

Set the oven heat to 350°F (175°C).

In a medium sized bowl, mix in the mashed bananas, rolled oats, almond butter, dark chocolate chips, and finally the vanilla extract.

Place spoonful on a baking sheet and then bake for about 15 minutes.

You can store this dish in a refrigerator for some days.

Put them in air tight containers

Nutritional Value:

Calories: 160

Protein: 4g

Fiber:

Preparation Time: 15 minutes

26. Berry Crisp with Almond Topping

This berry crisp recipe is simple dessert at its finest.

Ingredients:

- Two cups of mixed berries (e.g., blueberries, strawberries)
- One cup of old-fashioned oats
- Half cup of almond flour
- One quarter cup of maple syrup
- Two tablespoons of coconut oil

Preparation:

Set the oven heat to 375°F (190°C).

The proceed to put the mixed berries in a baking dish.

In a medium sized bowl, mix in the oats, almond flour, maple syrup, and melted coconut oil together.

Then spread the oat mixture evenly over the berries and bake for about 30 minutes.

Nutritional Value:

Calories: 220

Protein: 5g

Fiber: 8g

Preparation Time: 37 minutes

27. Dark Chocolate-Dipped Strawberries

This dark chocolate covered strawberries recipe make a great fancy desert and a delicious treat for seniors and every member of the family

Ingredients:

- ✓ One cup of fresh strawberries. Wash and dry them
- ✓ One quarter cup of dark chocolate chips

Preparation:

Wash and rinse the strawberries in water.

Then dip of the strawberry into the chocolate that is already melted.

Allow the excess to drip off.

Place them on a parchment paper-lined tray. Then go ahead to put them in a refrigerator until the chocolate becomes hard.

Nutritional Value:

Calories: 120

Fiber: 3g

Antioxidants: Cocoa in dark chocolate

Preparation Time: 18 minutes

28. Baked Apples with Cinnamon

If you are looking for a short cut way to eat apple pie, this is it

You will love the taste of this recipe.

And it is very nutritious

Ingredients:

- ✓ Four apples. Core and then cut into halves
- ✓ One quarter cup of chopped nuts (e.g., walnuts, almonds)
- ✓ Two tablespoons of honey
- ✓ One teaspoon of cinnamon

Preparation:

Set the oven heat to 375°F (190°C).

Place the apple that has been cut into halves in a baking dish.

In a medium-sized bowl, mix the chopped nuts, honey, and cinnamon together.

Then use your spoon to place the mixture into the apple halves.

Bake for about 25 minutes or until the apples becomes soft.

Nutritional Value:

Calories: 180

Protein: 3g

Fiber: 5g

Preparation Time: 35 minutes

29. Quinoa and Vegetable Stir-Fry

This quinoa stir fry is an Asian recipe, tasty and simple to make.

Most importantly, it is very nutritious and good for you.

Ingredients:

- ✓ One cup of quinoa, cooked
- ✓ Two cups of mixed vegetables (e.g., bell peppers, broccoli, snap peas)
- ✓ Two tablespoons of low-sodium soy sauce
- ✓ One tablespoon of sesame oil

Preparation:

In a frying pan, heat sesame oil over high heat.

Add the mixed vegetables and stir-fry until it becomes soft.

Add the cooked quinoa and then the soy sauce. Saute them

Toss until it mixes very well.

Nutritional Value:

Calories: 210

Protein: 12g

Fiber: 8g

Preparation Time: 22 minutes

30. Grilled Shrimp and Asparagus Skewers

Ingredients:

- ✓ Half pound of shrimp. Peel and devein them
- ✓ One bunch of asparagus. Trim them
- ✓ Two tablespoons of olive oil

- ✓ One lemon. Juice it
- ✓ One teaspoon of garlic powder
- ✓ Include salt and pepper to taste

Preparation:

Set the grill heat to medium-high heat level.

In a medium-sized bowl, toss the shrimp and asparagus with olive oil, lemon juice, garlic powder, salt, and pepper.

Thread the shrimp nicely by removing the dark colored membrane.

Then add it and the asparagus onto skewers and grill for about 8 minutes.

Nutritional Value:

Calories: 180

Protein: 22g

Omega-3 Fatty Acids: 0.5g

Preparation Time: 17 minutes

31. Sweet Potato and Black Bean Quesadillas

This recipe is easy to make in any quantity of your choice.

Ingredients:

- Two medium sweet potatoes. Grate them
- One can of black beans. Drain and rinse it
- One cup of shredded cheese (e.g., cheddar or Monterey Jack)
- Four whole wheat tortillas
- One teaspoon of cumin
- Salsa for serving (optional)

Preparation:

In a frying pan, cook the grated sweet potatoes until it becomes soft.

Add the black beans and cumin. Cook until it thoroughly heated.

Put a tortilla in the frying pant, add a layer of sweet potato mixture and cheese. Then top it with another tortilla.

Cook until the cheese get melted and tortillas become golden color.

Repeat the entire process for the remaining quesadillas.

Serve the dish with salsa if you want.

Nutritional Value:

Calories: 320

Protein: 15g

Fiber: 8g

Preparation Time: 27 minutes

32. Cucumber and Dill Greek Salad

Ingredients:

- Two cucumbers. Dice them
- One cup of cherry tomatoes. Cut them into halves
- Half cup of Kalamata olives. Slice it
- Half cup of feta cheese. Crumble it
- Two tablespoons of olive oil
- One tablespoon of red wine vinegar
- One tablespoon of fresh dill. Chop it nicely

Preparation:

In a large-sized bowl, mix up the diced cucumbers, cherry tomatoes, olives, and the feta cheese.

In another smaller bowl, stir together the olive oil, red wine vinegar, and the fresh dill.

Lavishly Sprinkle the dressing over the salad and toss until it is thoroughly coated.

Nutritional Value:

Calories: 180

Protein: 6g

Fiber: 5g

Preparation Time: 20 minutes

33. Berry and Almond Overnight Oats

Ingredients:

Half cup of rolled oats

Half cup of almond milk

One quarter cup of Greek yogurt

Half cup of mixed berries

One tablespoon of almond butter

One teaspoon of honey

Preparation:

In a jar, mix up the rolled oats, almond milk, Greek yogurt, and mixed berries.

Whisk them thoroughly.

Place a cover over it and refrigerate overnight.

At the breaking of dawn the next morning, top with almond butter and sprinkle honey over it before serving.

Nutritional Value:

Calories: 250

Protein: 10g

Fiber: 8g

Preparation Time: 5 minutes

34. Mediterranean Chickpea Salad

Enjoy this light easy lunch. Goes well for dinner as well

Ingredients:

- One can of chickpeas. Drain and rinse it
- One cucumber. Dice it
- One cup of cherry tomatoes. Cut it into halves
- One quarter cup of red onion. Chop it finely
- Two tablespoons of feta cheese. Crumble it
- Two tablespoons of olive oil
- One tablespoon of balsamic vinegar
- Fresh oregano to garnish it nicely

Preparation:

In a bowl, mix up the chickpeas, cucumber, tomatoes, red onion, and feta cheese together.

In another separate smaller sized bowl, stir the olive oil and balsamic vinegar together.

Drizzle the dressing over the salad and then toss in a gentle manner.

Then proceed to garnish the meal with fresh oregano before serving it.

Nutritional Value:

Calories: 250

Protein: 10g

Fiber: 8g

Preparation Time: 18 minutes

35. Spinach and Artichoke Stuffed Chicken Breast

This is a delicious dish is an excellent way to enjoy chicken breasts.

Ingredients:

- ✓ Two boneless, skinless chicken breasts
- ✓ One cup of fresh spinach. Chop it nicely
- ✓ Half cup of artichoke hearts. Chop it nicely
- ✓ One quarter cup of low-fat cream cheese
- ✓ One tablespoon of olive oil
- ✓ Include Salt and pepper to taste

Preparation:

Set the oven heat to 375°F (190°C).

Then in a medium-sized bowl, combine the chopped spinach, artichoke hearts, and cream cheese together.

Cut a small pocket into each of the chicken breast and then proceed to stuff it with the spinach and artichoke mixture.

Add salt and pepper to season the chicken.

Then bake the chicken for about 30 minutes.

Nutritional Value:

Calories: 280

Protein: 32g

Fiber: 5g

Preparation Time: 35 minutes

36. Cauliflower Fried Rice

This meal is a Chinese-style recipe. It is a healthy, low-carb dish that's hearty enough to serve as a side dish or even as a main course for you and the entire family.

Ingredients:

- ✓ One head of cauliflower. Grate it
- ✓ Two cups of mixed vegetables (e.g., peas, carrots, corn)
- ✓ Two eggs, beaten
- ✓ Two tablespoons of low-sodium soy sauce
- ✓ One tablespoon of sesame oil
- ✓ Green onions for garnish the meal

Preparation:

In a large-sized frying pan, stir-fry the mixed vegetables until they become soft.

Push the vegetables to one side. Add the beaten eggs to the empty side, and then scramble.

Mix up the grated cauliflower with the cooked vegetables and eggs.

whisk in the soy sauce and sesame oil.

Then go ahead to garnish with the green onions.

Nutritional Value:

Calories: 200

Protein: 12g

Fiber: 10g

Preparation Time: 20 minutes

37. Tomato Basil Mozzarella Salad

Ingredients:

- Two cups of cherry tomatoes. Cut into halves
- One cup of fresh mozzarella balls
- One quarter cup of fresh basil leaves, torn
- two tablespoons of balsamic glaze
- Include Salt and pepper to taste

Preparation:

In a medium-sized bowl, bring the cherry tomatoes, mozzarella balls, and torn basil leaves together and mix them properly.

Sprinkle the balsamic glaze and season it with salt and pepper.

Toss with gentle care before you serve.

Nutritional Value:

Calories: 220

Protein: 15g

Fiber: 3g

Preparation Time: 10 minutes

38. Salmon and Quinoa Stuffed Bell Peppers

Ingredients:

- Two bell peppers. Cut into halves
- One cup of cooked quinoa
- One pound of cooked salmon
- Two cans of pink salmon. Drain it
- Half cup of Greek yogurt
- 1 tablespoon of garlic powder
- One quarter cup of nicely chopped dill
- Include Lemon wedges for serving

Preparation:

Set the oven heat to 375°F (190°C).

Then in a medium sized bowl, combine the cooked quinoa, drained salmon, Greek yogurt, garlic powder and chopped dill together.

Then go ahead to stuff the bell pepper halves with the mixture and bake for another 25 minutes.

Proceed to serve with lemon wedges.

Nutritional Value:

Calories: 320

Protein: 30g

Fiber: 7g

Preparation Time: 30 minutes

39. Vegetarian Lentil Loaf

This meal is hearty, delicious and gluten-free

Ingredients:

- One cup of dried green lentils
- One onion. Chop it finely
- Two carrots. Grate them
- Half cup of breadcrumbs
- Two tablespoons of tomato paste
- One teaspoon of dried thyme

Preparation:

Cook the lentils according to the instructions from the package.

In a large-sized bowl, mix the cooked lentils, chopped onion, grated carrots, breadcrumbs, the tomato paste, and dried thyme together.

Proceed to press the entire mixture into a loaf pan and then bake it at a temperature of 375°F (190°C) for about 40 minutes.

Nutritional Value:

Calories: 210

Protein: 17g

Fiber: 12g

Preparation Time: 50 minutes

40. Cabbage and White Bean Soup

Easy to prepare and flavorful. You will really enjoy this.

Ingredients:

Half head of cabbage. Shred it

One can of white beans. Drain and rinse it

Two carrots. Slice them nicely

One onion. Dice it

Four cups of vegetable broth

One teaspoon of Italian seasoning.

Preparation:

In a large-sized pot, add the shredded cabbage, white beans, sliced carrots, diced onion, vegetable broth, and Italian seasoning together.

Over a medium heat, simmer for about 30 minutes until the vegetables becomes soft.

Nutritional Value:

Calories: 180

Protein: 10g

Fiber: 12g

Preparation Time: 35 minutes

BONUS RECIPE

41. Lemon Garlic Shrimp Pasta

Ingredients:

- ✓ Eight oz of whole grain spaghetti
- ✓ One pound of shrimp, peeled and deveined
- ✓ Three cloves of garlic. Mince it
- ✓ One lemon. Juice it
- ✓ Two tablespoons of olive oil
- ✓ Include Fresh parsley to garnish the dish

Preparation:

Start by cooking the whole grain spaghetti by following the instructions in the package.

In a medium-sized frying pan, gently fry the shrimp and minced garlic in olive oil until the shrimp becomes pink.

Move the cooked pasta from side to side with the shrimp mixture, add lemon juice, and garnish it with the fresh parsley.

Nutritional Value:

Calories: 350

Protein: 27g

Fiber: 7g

Preparation Time: 27 minutes

CONCLUSION

In the flavorful pages of this amazing cookbook - "Heart Healthy Diet Cookbook for Seniors," we've been to experiment and savor the sweet and healthy recipes to nourish not just the body, but the soul.

From the vibrant Mediterranean dish salads to the comforting warmth of lentil stews, each recipe is a testament to the joy of eating meals that are both hearty and healthy.

This cookbook isn't just about ingredients and making meals; it's a celebration of vitality, a dance of nutrients that whisper tales of well-being to your senior heart.

So, embrace the delicious combination of flavors, savor each of the bite, and let this collection of culinary wonders redefine what it means to eat well, live well, and love life.

I raise my glass to toast to health, happiness, and the irresistible magic of a heart-healthy feast!

Happy Feasting

30 Day Meal Planner

Weekly Meal Planner Journal

Dates

	BREAKFAST	LUNCH	DINNER	SNACKS
MON				
TUE				
WED				
THU				
FRI				
SAT				
SUN				

Shopping list

NOTES

Weekly Meal Planner Journal

Dates:

	BREAKFAST	LUNCH	DINNER	SNACKS
MON				
TUE				
WED				
THU				
FRI				
SAT				
SUN				

Shopping list
_____
_____
_____
_____
_____

NOTES

Weekly Meal Planner Journal

Dates

	BREAKFAST	LUNCH	DINNER	SNACKS
MON				
TUE				
WED				
THU				
FRI				
SAT				
SUN				

Shopping list

NOTES

Weekly Meal Planner Journal

Dates:

	BREAKFAST	LUNCH	DINNER	SNACKS
MON				
TUE				
WED				
THU				
FRI				
SAT				
SUN				

Shopping list

NOTES

Weekly Meal Planner Journal

Dates:

	BREAKFAST	LUNCH	DINNER	SNACKS
MON				
TUE				
WED				
THU				
FRI				
SAT				
SUN				

Shopping list

NOTES

Weekly Meal Planner Journal

Dates

	BREAKFAST	LUNCH	DINNER	SNACKS
MON				
TUE				
WED				
THU				
FRI				
SAT				
SUN				

Shopping list

_____
_____
_____
_____
_____

NOTES

Weekly Meal Planner Journal

Dates

	BREAKFAST	LUNCH	DINNER	SNACKS
MON				
TUE				
WED				
THU				
FRI				
SAT				
SUN				

Shopping list

NOTES

Weekly Meal Planner Journal

Dates

	BREAKFAST	LUNCH	DINNER	SNACKS
MON				
TUE				
WED				
THU				
FRI				
SAT				
SUN				

Shopping list

NOTES

Weekly Meal Planner Journal

Dates

	BREAKFAST	LUNCH	DINNER	SNACKS
MON				
TUE				
WED				
THU				
FRI				
SAT				
SUN				

Shopping list

NOTES

Weekly Meal Planner Journal

Dates:

	BREAKFAST	LUNCH	DINNER	SNACKS
MON				
TUE				
WED				
THU				
FRI				
SAT				
SUN				

Shopping list

NOTES

Weekly Meal Planner Journal

Dates:

	BREAKFAST	LUNCH	DINNER	SNACKS
MON				
TUE				
WED				
THU				
FRI				
SAT				
SUN				

Shopping list

NOTES

Weekly Meal Planner Journal

Dates

	BREAKFAST	LUNCH	DINNER	SNACKS
MON				
TUE				
WED				
THU				
FRI				
SAT				
SUN				

Shopping list

_____
_____
_____
_____
_____

NOTES

Weekly Meal planner Journal

Dates

	BREAKFAST	LUNCH	DINNER	SNACKS
MON				
TUE				
WED				
THU				
FRI				
SAT				
SUN				

Shopping list

NOTES

Weekly Meal Planner Journal

Dates:

	BREAKFAST	LUNCH	DINNER	SNACKS
MON				
TUE				
WED				
THU				
FRI				
SAT				
SUN				

Shopping list

NOTES

Weekly Meal Planner
Journal

Dates

	BREAKFAST	LUNCH	DINNER	SNACKS
MON				
TUE				
WED				
THU				
FRI				
SAT				
SUN				

Shopping list

NOTES

Weekly Meal Planner Journal

Dates

	BREAKFAST	LUNCH	DINNER	SNACKS
MON				
TUE				
WED				
THU				
FRI				
SAT				
SUN				

Shopping list

NOTES

Weekly Meal planner
Journal

Dates

	BREAKFAST	LUNCH	DINNER	SNACKS
MON				
TUE				
WED				
THU				
FRI				
SAT				
SUN				

Shopping list

NOTES

Weekly Meal Planner Journal

Dates:

	BREAKFAST	LUNCH	DINNER	SNACKS
MON				
TUE				
WED				
THU				
FRI				
SAT				
SUN				

Shopping list

NOTES

Weekly Meal Planner Journal

Dates

	BREAKFAST	LUNCH	DINNER	SNACKS
MON				
TUE				
WED				
THU				
FRI				
SAT				
SUN				

Shopping list

NOTES

WEEKLY MEAL PLANNER JOURNAL　　Dates

	BREAKFAST	LUNCH	DINNER	SNACKS
MON				
TUE				
WED				
THU				
FRI				
SAT				
SUN				

Shopping list

NOTES

Weekly Meal Planner Journal

Dates

	BREAKFAST	LUNCH	DINNER	SNACKS
MON				
TUE				
WED				
THU				
FRI				
SAT				
SUN				

Shopping list
_____
_____
_____
_____
_____

NOTES

WEEKLY MEAL PLANNER JOURNAL — Dates

	BREAKFAST	LUNCH	DINNER	SNACKS
MON				
TUE				
WED				
THU				
FRI				
SAT				
SUN				

Shopping list

NOTES

Weekly Meal Planner Journal

Dates

	BREAKFAST	LUNCH	DINNER	SNACKS
MON				
TUE				
WED				
THU				
FRI				
SAT				
SUN				

Shopping list

NOTES

Weekly Meal Planner Journal

Dates

	BREAKFAST	LUNCH	DINNER	SNACKS
MON				
TUE				
WED				
THU				
FRI				
SAT				
SUN				

Shopping list

NOTES

Weekly Meal Planner Journal

Dates

	BREAKFAST	LUNCH	DINNER	SNACKS
MON				
TUE				
WED				
THU				
FRI				
SAT				
SUN				

Shopping list

NOTES

WEEKLY MEAL PLANNER JOURNAL

Dates

	BREAKFAST	LUNCH	DINNER	SNACKS
MON				
TUE				
WED				
THU				
FRI				
SAT				
SUN				

Shopping list

NOTES

Weekly Meal Planner Journal

Dates

	BREAKFAST	LUNCH	DINNER	SNACKS
MON				
TUE				
WED				
THU				
FRI				
SAT				
SUN				

Shopping list

NOTES

Weekly Meal Planner Journal

Dates

	BREAKFAST	LUNCH	DINNER	SNACKS
MON				
TUE				
WED				
THU				
FRI				
SAT				
SUN				

Shopping list
_____
_____
_____
_____
_____

NOTES

Weekly Meal Planner Journal

Dates

	BREAKFAST	LUNCH	DINNER	SNACKS
MON				
TUE				
WED				
THU				
FRI				
SAT				
SUN				

Shopping list

NOTES

Weekly Meal Planner Journal

Dates:

	BREAKFAST	LUNCH	DINNER	SNACKS
MON				
TUE				
WED				
THU				
FRI				
SAT				
SUN				

Shopping list

NOTES

WEEKLY MEAL PLANNER
JOURNAL

Dates

	BREAKFAST	LUNCH	DINNER	SNACKS
MON				
TUE				
WED				
THU				
FRI				
SAT				
SUN				

Shopping list

NOTES

Weekly Meal Planner Journal

Dates

	BREAKFAST	LUNCH	DINNER	SNACKS
MON				
TUE				
WED				
THU				
FRI				
SAT				
SUN				

Shopping list

NOTES

Weekly Meal Planner Journal

Dates

	BREAKFAST	LUNCH	DINNER	SNACKS
MON				
TUE				
WED				
THU				
FRI				
SAT				
SUN				

Shopping list

NOTES

Weekly Meal Planner Journal

Dates

	BREAKFAST	LUNCH	DINNER	SNACKS
MON				
TUE				
WED				
THU				
FRI				
SAT				
SUN				

Shopping list

NOTES

Weekly Meal planner Journal

Dates

	BREAKFAST	LUNCH	DINNER	SNACKS
MON				
TUE				
WED				
THU				
FRI				
SAT				
SUN				

Shopping list

NOTES

THANK YOU

Printed in the USA
CPSIA information can be obtained
at www.ICGtesting.com
LVHW080557110724
785188LV00006B/347